Theatrum Scotiæ: containing the prospects of His Majesty's castles and palaces: together with those of the most considerable towns and colleges; ... ruins ... All curiously engraven on copper-plates. With a description of each place.

John Slezer

ECCO
PRINT EDITIONS

Theatrum Scotiæ: containing the prospects of His Majesty's castles and palaces: together with those of the most considerable towns and colleges; ... ruins ... All curiously engraven on copper-plates. With a description of each place.
Slezer, John
ESTCID: T084163
Reproduction from British Library
Anonymous. By John Slezer. The descriptions are based in part on Latin writings of Sir Robert Sibbald. With an engraved dedication leaf, signed: Andrew Johnston. Titlepage in red and black, identical to that of the other 1718 edition.
London : printed for D. Browne; J. Senex; W. Taylor; W. Mears, J. Browne, and F. Clay, and A. Johnston, 1718.
[2],12p.,plates ; 2°

Eighteenth Century
Collections Online
Print Editions

Gale ECCO Print Editions

Relive history with *Eighteenth Century Collections Online*, now available in print for the independent historian and collector. This series includes the most significant English-language and foreign-language works printed in Great Britain during the eighteenth century, and is organized in seven different subject areas including literature and language; medicine, science, and technology; and religion and philosophy. The collection also includes thousands of important works from the Americas.

The eighteenth century has been called "The Age of Enlightenment." It was a period of rapid advance in print culture and publishing, in world exploration, and in the rapid growth of science and technology – all of which had a profound impact on the political and cultural landscape. At the end of the century the American Revolution, French Revolution and Industrial Revolution, perhaps three of the most significant events in modern history, set in motion developments that eventually dominated world political, economic, and social life.

In a groundbreaking effort, Gale initiated a revolution of its own: digitization of epic proportions to preserve these invaluable works in the largest online archive of its kind. Contributions from major world libraries constitute over 175,000 original printed works. Scanned images of the actual pages, rather than transcriptions, recreate the works ***as they first appeared.***

Now for the first time, these high-quality digital scans of original works are available via print-on-demand, making them readily accessible to libraries, students, independent scholars, and readers of all ages.

For our initial release we have created seven robust collections to form one the world's most comprehensive catalogs of 18th century works.

Initial Gale ECCO Print Editions collections include:

> ***History and Geography***
> Rich in titles on English life and social history, this collection spans the world as it was known to eighteenth-century historians and explorers. Titles include a wealth of travel accounts and diaries, histories of nations from throughout the world, and maps and charts of a world that was still being discovered. Students of the War of American Independence will find fascinating accounts from the British side of conflict.

Social Science

Delve into what it was like to live during the eighteenth century by reading the first-hand accounts of everyday people, including city dwellers and farmers, businessmen and bankers, artisans and merchants, artists and their patrons, politicians and their constituents. Original texts make the American, French, and Industrial revolutions vividly contemporary.

Medicine, Science and Technology

Medical theory and practice of the 1700s developed rapidly, as is evidenced by the extensive collection, which includes descriptions of diseases, their conditions, and treatments. Books on science and technology, agriculture, military technology, natural philosophy, even cookbooks, are all contained here.

Literature and Language

Western literary study flows out of eighteenth-century works by Alexander Pope, Daniel Defoe, Henry Fielding, Frances Burney, Denis Diderot, Johann Gottfried Herder, Johann Wolfgang von Goethe, and others. Experience the birth of the modern novel, or compare the development of language using dictionaries and grammar discourses.

Religion and Philosophy

The Age of Enlightenment profoundly enriched religious and philosophical understanding and continues to influence present-day thinking. Works collected here include masterpieces by David Hume, Immanuel Kant, and Jean-Jacques Rousseau, as well as religious sermons and moral debates on the issues of the day, such as the slave trade. The Age of Reason saw conflict between Protestantism and Catholicism transformed into one between faith and logic -- a debate that continues in the twenty-first century.

Law and Reference

This collection reveals the history of English common law and Empire law in a vastly changing world of British expansion. Dominating the legal field is the *Commentaries of the Law of England* by Sir William Blackstone, which first appeared in 1765. Reference works such as almanacs and catalogues continue to educate us by revealing the day-to-day workings of society.

Fine Arts

The eighteenth-century fascination with Greek and Roman antiquity followed the systematic excavation of the ruins at Pompeii and Herculaneum in southern Italy; and after 1750 a neoclassical style dominated all artistic fields. The titles here trace developments in mostly English-language works on painting, sculpture, architecture, music, theater, and other disciplines. Instructional works on musical instruments, catalogs of art objects, comic operas, and more are also included.

THEATRUM SCOTIÆ:

CONTAINING THE

PROSPECTS

OF HIS MAJESTY's

CASTLES and PALACES:

Together with thoſe of the

Moſt Conſiderable TOWNS and COLLEGES;

The RUINS of many Ancient

Abbeys, Churches, Monaſteries, and *Convents*

Within the ſaid KINGDOM

All Curiouſly Engraven on COPPER-PLATES.

With a DESCRIPTION of each PLACE.

John Slezer

LONDON Printed for *D Browne* at *Exeter-Change*, *J Senex* in *Salisbury Court*, *W Taylor* in *Pater noſter-Row*, *W Mears*, *J Browne*, and *F Clay* near *Temple-Bar*, and *A Johnſton* at *Round-Court* in the *Strand* MDCCXVIII.

The following Prospects of ye Pallaces

are Most humbly Inscribed

To his Royal Highness

The Prince of Wales

By his Most humble and Most Obedient Servant

Andrew Johnston

Theatrum SCOTIÆ.

E D I N B U R G H.

EDINBURGH is ſituated in *Mid-Lothian*, a Shire of *Scotland* It is the chief City of the Kingdom, and the Royal Seat It far ſurpaſſeth all the other Cities of the Kingdom in the Statelineſs of its Churches, the Beauty and Neatneſs of its publick and private Buildings, the Largneſs of its Precincts, the Number and Opulency of its Inhabitants, and Dignity of its Rulers. By the moſt ancient Inhabitants it was called *Dun Eden*, by the *Latins*, *Edinodunum*, and by the *Germans*, *Edinburghen*, all which ſignifie the ſame thing

Dun Eden ſignifies a Town upon a Hill, or rather a City of the *Edeni*, ſituated on a Hill The *Edeni* are thoſe who by *Ptolomy* are termed *Ottodeni*, which Word (as ſome Learned Men think) was miſtaken for *Scottodeni*, the two firſt Letters *Sc* being worn out with Time For near to this City is *Curia Ottodenorum*, whoſe Name remains to this Day in a Village four Miles Weſt from the City, called *Curre* And two Miles Weſt from the Town is *Corſtopitum* (which alſo was among the *Ottodeni*) which is a Village commonly called *Coſto fi*

Ptolomy calls this Place Στρατόπεδον πτερωτόν, *Caſtrum alatum*, the *Winged Caſtle*, which is not ſo called from that kind of Wings, which the *Greek* Builders (as ſays *Vitruvius*) call πτερώματα, (which are double Walls ſo riſing to the Height, that they reſemble Wings For it is likely there was no regular Building in this Place at that time) but that they were ſuch as by the Poet *Juvenal* are called *Caſtella Brigantum*, which ſort of Caſtles we may ſee deſcribed by *Tacitus*, *Annal Lib* XII where he ſays, That upon high Mountains, and other Places of difficult Acceſs, they build up Stones in Form of a Fence, where the River did run on a ſlippery Ford Now theſe Fences of Stone were nothing elſe, but Stones caſt together without Mortar, which is alſo clear from the ſame Author in the forecited Place, where he ſays, The Soldiers holding their Bucklers over their Heads for a Defence, pulled down the unwrought and ill-built Stones, which could not have been ſo eaſily done, if they had not been caſt together without Mortar And certainly our Anceſtors choſe out this as a very fit Place for a Fort of that Nature For the Hill where the Caſtle ſtands is exceeding ſteep and craggy, and the Aſcent very difficult, except where it looks to the Eaſt, which Part they fortified with Stones caſt together as before The Aſcent on which the City now ſtands, had, and yet hath upon the North Side, a ſtanding Pool, which is commonly called the *North Loch* or Lake Upon the South Side of the Hill there was likewiſe another ſtanding Pool, called the *South Loch* The Verity of which the Rights and Leaſes of ſome Houſes of St *Ninian's* Row doth teſtifie, which are let with the Privilege of a Boat annexed, and theſe two *Lochs* or Lakes bounded the City upon theſe two Sides, as the *North Loch* does at this Day upon the North Side, but the *South Loch* was drained a Hundred Years ago, and upon the Banks thereof are built two ſeveral Tracts of Houſes, between which (in the Place where the *Loch* it ſelf ſtood) is a Street called the *Cowgate* And ſo the Breadth of the City toward the South, is far extended beyond its former Limits, as likewiſe the Length thereof toward the Weſt is much enlarged, for the Graſs-Market and Horſe-Market are now within the City-Wall

The Reaſon why this Place was called *Caſtrum Alatum*, or *The Winged Caſtle*, is to be taken from the very Nature of the Place For beſides the Lakes on both Sides, there are two Hills near the Rock on which the Caſtle ſtands, *viz.*, *Sarisbury* and *Neils Craigs*, or Rocks, ſo named from the ſometime Owners thereof, which in a manner reſemble Wings, as is eaſily perceived by thoſe who come to the City from the South-Eaſt by the Sea-ſide, for then theſe Rocks appear like Wings ſtretched forth, and the Rock on which the Caſtle ſtands, like the Head of a Bird with a Tuft. And this is the genuine Derivation of the Word

I know there are ſome Learned Perſons who will have *Ptolomy's Caſtrum Alatum* to be another Part of the Country, and not to be *Edinodunum*, ſeeing he makes his Στρατόπεδον to be amongſt the *Vacomagi*; but *Ptolomy* muſt be born with in all his Miſtakes of the Situation of Places here, for being an *Egyptian*, living in *Alexandria*, and forced to take Things upon Truſt, and follow the Relation of others, it is no Wonder if he be ſometimes miſtaken

The greater Part of the City is built upon the Aſcent, and it is very probable that the Caſtle has been the Cauſe of building the City For firſt the Neighbours have built a few Houſes near the Caſtle, that under the Reach thereof they might be defended from the Injuries of their Enemies The Number of the People growing apace, the Number of the Houſes likewiſe encreaſed, and ſtretched forth by the very Foot of the Aſcent towards the Eaſt, by which the City, together with the Suburbs of the *Canongate* and King's Palace, is become one entire *Scotch* Mile in Length, but in Breadth it is leſs by the Half, notwithſtanding the Suburbs be included The High Street, from the Caſtle to the Abby, is adorned with ſtately Buildings, which are of late made of hewen Stone, ſince by an Act of the Town-Council it hath been prohibited (becauſe of the frequent Fires which happened) to build any more Timber-Houſes either in the City or Suburbs

The great Breadth of the High-Street, and of the many Lanes which lye on each ſide the ſame, from the North to the South (which ſend up the Air as it were by Pipes into the High-Street) and the Neatneſs of the two Hills called *Neils Craigs* on the North, and *Sarisbury Craigs* on the South, do always refresh the Town with Air, which conduces not a little to the Wholesomeness hereof, and it was never heard that the Plague raged in it, except brought in thither by infected Wares. Which Purity of the Air is daily encreased since the Time that excellent fresh Water was brought into the City from a Fountain three Miles distant from the same, and that by a most wise Act of the Council all Nastiness is removed.

The City is enclosed with a kind of an old *Roman* Wall on every Side, except towards the North, where the *North Loch* does secure it instead of a Wall.

The City is entered by six Gates or Ports, two of which are to the East, two to the South, one to the West, and one lately made to the North.

One of the Gates to the East is called the *Netherbow*, which in the Year 1616 was magnificently rebuilt, being the chief Gate of the City, adorned with Towers on both Sides

The other Gate to the East is called the *Cowgate-Port*, through which there is an Entry into the Nether Street, of the Length of the whole City, and is called the *Cowgate*

The Eastmost of these Gates to the South (through which is an Entry into the City) is called the *Potter-Row Port*, from the Suburb called the *Potter-Row*.

The Westmost of these is called the *Society-Port*, properly the *Brewer's-Port* They have a great Square Court in that Place, with Buildings and brave Houses round about it to the very Walls of the City.

The West Gate at the other End of the City, lying beneath the Castle, affords an Entry from the Suburb of the same Name

The North Gate, which was last made at the lower End of the *North Loch*, is two-fold the Inner and the Outer Port, through which there is an Entry into the City from the Suburb called the *Mutter's Hill*.

There are two Streets extending the whole Length of the Town The chief Street, which is also called the Higher, is one of the broadest in *Europe* From it there run many Lanes, here called Winds, on both Sides The Nether or Lower Street hath also many Lanes running to the South.

In the very Middle of the City there is a Cathedral Church, which is called St *Giles's* Church, of such Largeness that it is divided into four Churches, every one of which has its own Parish. It is built of hewen Stone, adorned with Pillars and *Vaultings* of Stone In the Middle it forms a perfect Cross, by four Parts of this Church meeting together, and they support a stately high Tower, with a Top of curious Workmanship, representing an Imperial Crown Beside this Cathedral Church, there are in the City,

The South Church, called the *Gray-Friars* Church, which stands in the Middle of the common Burial-place. Many Tombs and Monuments do surround the Church-yard, amongst which that of Sir *George Mackenzy*, Lord-Advocate or Attorney-General to King *Charles* and King *James* the Second, does appear like a *Mausoleum*

There is also a Church of square hewen Stone with a Tower, built in the Year 1641, which is called the *Trone* Church

The Collegiate-Church of the *Sacred Trinity* was built by *Mary* of *Gueldres*, King *James* the Second's Queen, where also she lies interred.

Near to this Church is the Hospital of St *Thomas*, in which the poorer Sort of Inhabitants, both Men and Women, are maintained splendidly enough, and have their own proper Chaplain

Over-against this Church is the *Correction-House*, commonly called *Paul's-Work*, in which there are divers Manufactures of Linnen, Wooll, and Silk, where dissolute Persons are forced to earn their Living by their Labour

The Lady *Yester's* Church, was built by one of the Lady *Yesters*, who also left a Sum of Money for maintaining a good and able Man to preach and perform Divine Service therein

Besides these Churches there are two Chapels in the City, that of St. *Magdalen's* in the *Cowgate*, and St. *Mary's* in *Niddries Wind* There is another Chapel of the same Name at the Foot of the *Cannon-gate*, as likewise several *Meeting-Houses* lately built, both in the City and Suburbs

About the Middle of the *Cannon-Gate*, upon the North Side of it, there is built, within these five Years, a very beautiful Church, and a considerable Piece of Ground inclosed for a Church-yard, by a Mortification made by Sir *Thomas Mooate* of *Sachten-Hall* for that Purpose

Near unto the Cathedral Church is the *Parliament-House*, where the Three Estates of the Kingdom did convene It stands in a great Court, the North Side whereof is bounded by the Church it self, the West Side is enclosed by the Council-House, where the Town-Council assembles, the South Side enclosed by the Sessions-House, where the Judges and Lords of Session sit to give Justice to the People. In the upper Part of this Building are the Privy-Council and Exchequer-Chambers The rest of the South and East Side of this Court is inclosed with the upper and lower Exchange, and with a Tract of most stately Buildings Here is one of the highest Houses in the World, mounting seven Stories above the Parliament Court, and being built upon a great Descent of the Hill, the Back Part of it is as far below it, so that from the Bottom to the Top one Stair-case ascends fourteen Stories high

In the Middle of the Court is the Statue of King *Charles* the Second in Brass, erected upon a stately Pedestal at the Charge of the City of *Edinburgh*

About twenty Years ago the said Magistrates were at a vast Expence also to bring one of the best Springs in *Scotland* into this City by Leaden Pipes from a Hill about three Miles distant from it; and they have erected several stately Fountains in the Middle of the High Street to serve the Town with Water

In *Gray's Close* near the *Netherbow*, is the *Mint-House*, with a large Court, adorned with most neat and convenient Buildings, for Accommodation of the Overseers and Workmen thereunto belonging.

Upon the South Side is the College of King *James* the Sixth, founded in the Year 1580, endowed with all the Privileges of an University It hath most large Precincts enclosed with Walls, and divided into three Courts, two lower, and one higher, which is equal to both the other in Largeness These Courts or *Area's* are adorned on all Sides with excellent Buildings. There is also a high Tower built over the great Entry

The publick Schools are large There is likewise a very large Common-Hall, in which Theology and the *Hebrew* Tongue is taught, and publick Orations made There is a Library with all sorts of Books, and some Manuscripts. Under the Library is the King's *Printing-House*.

There is a very good Accommodation for the Students, and neat and handsome Dwellings for the Professors, with very fine Gardens for their Recreation.

The *Castle* is situated at the Head of the Town to the West, where the Hill doth rise into a large Top It is a very Ἀκρόπολις, for it both hangs over and commands the Town The Rock on which the Castle is situated is upon the South, West, and North inaccessible. The Entry to the Castle is from the Town. The chief Defence on this Side is a round Battery, at the Foot of which there is a designed Out-Work, which is not yet brought to a Condition of Defence, and will add very much to the Strength of it when finish'd. In the Castle also is a Royal Palace of hewen Stone, where the *Regalia* of the Kingdom are kept. This Castle is the chief Magazine for the Arms and Ammunition of the Nation, and hath a most pleasant Prospect to the neighbouring Fields, and to the River of *Forth*, from whence it is saluted by such Ships of War as come to an Anchor in *Leith* Road The Governour of this Fortress is generally a Nobleman in favour with the Government.

Heriot's Hospital is likewise within the City, situated to the West of the publick Burial-Place It is a Nursery for Boys, in which the Citizens Children who are poor are brought up, under the Tutelage of a Governour, who, according to the Constitution of the Founder, is to live single They have likewise a Chaplain to instruct them in the Grounds of Learning, 'till they be fitted for the publick Schools and Colleges

This Hospital was founded by *George Heriot*, Jeweller to King *James* the Sixth, who was descended of the Family of *Trebroun*, and after he had lost two Sons by Shipwreck going from *Scotland* to *London*, where dying without Issue *February* the 15th, 1624, he left in Legacy to this Hospital Two Hundred Thousand Pounds *Scots* Money, that Youth might be maintained therein, and instructed in Arts and Sciences 'till they were of mature Age, having left the City of *Edinburgh* his Executors

This Fabrick is stately like a Palace, the Statue of the Founder being erected upon the inner Frontispiece Round about the Houses are most pleasant Gardens, adorn'd with large Walks and pleasant Greens

Without the Walls of the City are the Suburbs, amongst which that which lies from the *Nethe bow* to the Abbey, called the *Cannon-Gate*, hath the Preheminence It is adorned with goodly Buildings and fine Gardens Upon the North Side of it is the *Tolbooth*, where the Bailiffs of the same do convene for the Administration of Justice. On the South Side is a very fine House belonging to the Earl of *Murray*, with pleasant Gardens adjoining.

At the lower End of this Suburb is the Abbey of *Holyrude-House*, founded by King *David* for the Monks of the Order of St. *Augustine* This was consumed by Fire, and the Church only remains, in which divers Kings and Queens are interred

The *Royal Palace* hath four Courts The outer Court, which is as big as all the rest, hath four principal Entries (besides several Inlets into the adjacent Gardens) three of which are on the West, and the other on the East Side

The Entry of the Palace is adorned with great Pillars of hewen Stone, and a fine Cupula in Fashion of a Crown above it. The Fore-part of the Palace is terminated by four high Towers, two of which toward the North were erected by King *James* the Fifth, and the rest by King *Charles* the Second. The Fabrick of the Inner Court is very stately, with *Piazza's* round about it, all of fine hewen Stone. From these covered Walks you have Access to the several Apartments which are most Royal and Magnificent But above all, the long Gallery is remarkable, being adorn'd with the Pictures of the Kings of *Scotland* from *Fergus* the First.

The Palace on all Hands is bounded with lovely Gardens On the South lies the King's Park, which hath great Variety of Medicinal Plants Here also is an admirable Fountain, which through Conduits serves the whole House His Grace the Duke of *Hamilton* is Hereditary Keeper of this Palace

De *EDINBURGO*, *JOHANNIS JONSTONI* Carmen

Monte sub acclivi Zephyri procurrit in auras.
Hinc arx celsa, illinc Regia clara nitet
Inter utramque patet sublimibus ardua tectis
Urbs armis, animis clara, frequensque viris
Nobile Scotorum *caput, & pars maxima regni,*
Pene etiam gentis integra regna suæ
Raræ artes & ope, quod mens optaverit, aut hic*
Invenias, aut non Scotia *tota dabit*
Compositum hic populum videas sanctumque senatum
Sanctaque cum puro lumine jura Dei
An quisquam Arctoi *extremo in limite mundi*
Aut hac, aut paria his cernere posse putet?
Dic, Hospes, postquam externas lustraveris oras,
Hæc cernens oculis credis an ipse tuis?

DUNBRITTON.

DUMBARTON, or *Dunbritton*, is a Town in the Sheriffdom of *Lenox*, which *Beda* calls *Allclyth*, others *Allcluith* It has its Name from *Dun*, which in our ancient Language signifies a Hill or Rock, and *Bar*, which in the same Language signifies the Top or Height of any thing. The Town is situate in a Plain on the Bank of the River *Levin*, near the Place where it enters into *Clyde*, a little below the Castle, which is excellently fortified by Nature, owing little to Art, and seems to have been built by the ancient *Brigantes* This Town had its Privileges procured to it by one of the Countesses of *Lennox*

The Castle hath a strange kind of Situation, for where the Waters of *Clyde* and *Levin* meet, there's a Plain extended to the Length of a Mile at the Foot of the neighbouring Hills: And in the very Corner where the Rivers meet there rises a Rock with two Tops, the higher of which looks to the West, with a Watch-tower on the top of it, having a large Prospect on all Sides. The other, being a little lower, lyes to the East Betwixt these two Tops are Steps hewen out of the Rock with great Pains and Labour, which yield Passage only to one Person at a time, to the Upper-part of the Castle To the South where *Clyde* runs by the Rock, which is naturally steep, it hath a little Descent, and, as it were with out-stretch'd Arms, embraces the plain Ground, which, partly by Nature, and partly by Art, is so enclosed, that it furnishes Room for several Houses and a Garden. It secures the Harbour by its Ordnance;

nance, and obliges the smaller Boats to come up almost to the very Gate of the Castle, the Channel of the River running on that side. The Middle of the Rock, where the Entry to the Castle is, being built up with Houses, makes as it were another Castle distinct from the former. This Castle, as appears by its Prospects, does almost stand like a Sugar-loaf upon a plain Ground. The Circumference of it is but very small, and yet it hath at the top a little kind of a Lake and several other Springs Besides the natural Fortification, it is bounded on the West by the Water of *Levin*, and on the South by *Clyde*, which are to it instead of Ditches. To the East the Sea, at a full Tide, beats against the Foot of the Rock; and when it ebbs it does not leave a Plain of Sand, but of a soft Clay, which is divided by a Rivulet that runs down from the neighbouring Hills. The Town gives Title of Earl to a Branch of the Noble Family of *Douglas*

STIRLING.

STIRLING is the chief Town of the Shire of that Name, where the Sheriff keeps his Courts. It hath its Name from its Situation, for the Town stands upon the Descent of a steep Rock, at the Foot of which there runs a deep River call'd *Boderia*, or *Bodotria*, or *Forth* It takes its Name from the *Saxon* Word *Ster*, which signifies a Hill, and *Lin* a Water

It was of old called *Binobara*, which by some is judged to be *Ptolomy's Vindovara* For *Bin* in our old Language signifies a Hill, and *Vara* a River. So that the Name which the Town now retains, is the Signification of the old Name thereof

At the Head of the Town stands a well fortified Castle, adorned with stately Buildings in the former Age by King *James* the Fifth This is the Place, as *Tacitus* observes, where *Clyde* and *Forth* are divided from one another by a small Neck of Land, which was then strengthened by a Wall and Garrisons; and all that *Isthmus* possessed by Soldiers, the Enemies being removed as it were into another Island, the Inscription on a Stone below the Castle toward the Bridge, which makes mention of a Wing of the Army that kept Watch there, seeming to intimate as much And although the *Romans* did several times infest some Places beyond it by their Inroads, yet the Strength and Glory of the *Roman* Name had its Boundary in this Place

The King's Park lies at the very Foot of the Castle, and the City stands on the Back of a Hill toward the South. It is enclosed with a Wall, and toward the North it is bounded with the River *Forth*, which is crossed by a Bridge in that Place.

The Bridge is of hewen Stone, and fortified with an Iron Gate. It consists of four stately Arches, and lies South and North

The Ships at full Tide come up to the Bridge, and the Haven is a little below the same.

The Church, which is of hewen Stone built very artificially, stands in the upper Part of the Town toward the East, adorned with a very high Tower

Not far from the Church may be seen the Mansions of the Earls of *Argyle* and *Marr*, notable both for their Bigness and the Artifice of their Structure

The Earl of *Marr* was Governour of this Castle by Heritage It hath a competent Number of great Ordnance for defending the Passage of the Bridge, and a sufficient Garrison established for its Security.

In times of Trouble the chief Magazine of the Nation is usually transported to this Place, it lying upon a considerable Pass, and almost in the Center of the Kingdom

As this City stands in a most commodious Place for Commerce, so it hath a most delectable and pleasant Prospect, by the great and various Windings of the River *Forth*, which are so extraordinary, that from the Bridge of *Stirling* to the Town of *Allowa*, it is twenty four Miles by Land, and but four by Water

ALLOWA, a Town in *Clackmannan-shire*, which seems to be the same *Ptolomy* calls *Alauna*, is situated on a pleasant Plain to the North of *Forth*, and hath a convenient Harbour for Ships of Burthen, many of which come thither for Salt and Coals Here the Earl of *Marr*, Chief of the *Areskins*, hath a pleasant Dwelling with a Wood adjacent

De STERLINO, J JONSTONI
Carmen

Regia sublimis celsa despectat ab arce
Pendula, sub bifertis mœnia structa jugis.
Regum augusta Parens, Regum nutricula natis,
Hinc sibi Regifico nomine tota placet.
Hospita sed cunctis, quovis sub nomine, amicus
Sive es, seu non es, Hospes an Hostis item
Pro lucro cedit damnum, discordia tristis
Heu quoties procerum sanguine tinxit humum!
Hoc uno infœlix, at fœlix cætera, nusquam
Lætior aut cœli frons, geniusve soli

LINLITHGOW.

IS the same which *Ptolomy* calls *Lindum*, so named for its being situated on the Side of a Lake. The King's Palace stands on a little Hill, towards the Middle of the said Lake, in which there lies an Island, which ascends with several Steps, in the Form of an Amphitheatre This Palace is magnificently built of hewen Stone, begun by former Kings, and perfected by King *James* the Sixth

It consists of four Towers, between which the Court, the Chapel, and the rest of the Buildings are extended. The Porch bears the Name and Arms of King *James* the Fifth. In the inner Court there is a very artificial Fountain, adorned with several Statues and Water-Works

Close by the Palace is a Church, commonly called St. *Michael's*, of a most excellent Structure, with a very high Steeple, to which the late Earl of *Linlithgow* added an extraordinary neat Chapel There is a small and easie Descent from the Palace to the Town, where is to be seen a large four-square Court, in the Middle of which there is another curious Fountain, exceeding in all Respects that which is in the inner Court of the Palace.

On the South Side of this Court is the *Tolbooth*, which is very neatly built of hewen Stone, having a very high Steeple with Bells, and a very fine Clock. In this *Tolbooth* the Sheriff and Town-Magistrates keep their Courts

There

There is a large Street reaches from the one End of the Town to the other, which is adorned on every Side with fair Buildings, from each Side of which Street divers Lanes do break out, whish open a Passage into several pleasant Gardens

The Lake it self is a Mile in Length, and a Quarter of a Mile over, and abounds with Perch, and other sorts of Fish On the North Side hereof lies the King's Park

This Town hath a Harbour for all sorts of Ships near the Castle of *Blackness*, where there is a large Custom-House built, with other Houses for the Use of Merchants

The Earl of *Linlithgow* is Hereditary Keeper of the Palace, and the King's Baily in that Place

De LIMNUCHO, Carmen ARCTURI JONSTONI

Nobile Limnuchum *est, Pario de marmore templum*
Hic nitet, impensæ non mediocris opus.
Æmula sunt templi turrita palatia Regis,
Et Pratio superant Solis *utramque domum*
Proximus est urbi nullo lacus aggere cinctus,
Squammiger illimes Grex natat inter aquas.
Ista triumphales præbent vivaria cænas
Grampiaco quoties sub Jove *miles ovat*
Regius hic lacus est Lucrinus, Cæsaris *unda*
Plus habet hic luxus, plus habet ille dapes

FALKLAND.

FALKLAND is a pretty large Town in the Sheriffdom of *Fife* At the Foot of *Lomon* Hill, there is a stately Palace, which King *James* the Fifth caused to be built for a retiring Place, it being most convenient also for Hunting

The King's Park and a Wood are adjacent to it, into which, as also into the Plain toward the East, it hath the most pleasant Prospect The Duke of *Athol* is Hereditary Keeper of this Palace, and hath a considerable Rent by the neighbouring Lands and Stewartry It gives Title of *Viscount* to the Family of *Falkland*, a Branch of the *English* Family of *Cary*

St. ANDREWS.

ST ANDRREWS, in Latin *Andreanopolis*, or *Fanum Sancti Andreæ*, has its Name from St. *Andrew*, whose Bones are said to be brought hither from *Patras*, a Town in *Peloponnesus*, by *Regulus*, a *Grecian* Monk, *Anno* 368, a Man in that Age much esteem d for Piety, as appears by the Church dedicated to him, and called after his Name From him also (as ancient Writers report) this Town was at first called *Regimund*, that is *Mons Sancti Reguli*, for we read that *Oengus*, or *Ungus*, King of the *Picts*, did grant to *God* and St *Andrew*, That he should be Head of all the Churches within the Jurisdiction of the *Picts*

Likewise it is manifest from old Manuscripts, that this was the principal Seat of the *Culdees*, who had the Care and Management of Holy Things from the first Reception of Christianity in those Parts

This City was the *Metropolis* of the whole Kingdom and the See of an Archbishop, who was Primate of all *Scotland* It lies toward the East, with a pleasant Prospect to the Ocean, having a Harbour for Ships, the Sea near it plentiful in Fishes, and Fields wholsome and spacious.

There yet remain the Marks of venerable Antiquity, the Ruins of the Cathedral Church and Monastery, which do abundantly testifie their ancient Glory and Magnificence The Town it self is situate in a Plain, from East to West, with a most pleasant Prospect to the *German* Ocean It had a very strong Castle of old, whose Rubbish and Ruins are yet to be seen upon the Rocks on the Sea-side towards the North It has Streets straight and broad, stretching East and West, whereof two lead to that once famous Abbey of *Canons Regular* of the Order of St *Augustine*, situate toward the East and South-East, the Wall surrounding this Abbey being yet entire, and of hewen Stone, with many Towers and Turrets, which give it the Resemblance of a King's Palace

The chief Church in the Town now, is that called the *New Church*, not far from the *New College* In it there is to be seen a very magnificent Monument of Archbishop *Sharp*.

There is also another Church, St *Leonard's*, adjacent to a College of the same Name, the Rector whereof is ordinarily the Principal of the said College, but the greatest Ornament of this City is the University, the *Athens* of *Scotland*, consisting at present of three Colleges, and was first founded by *Laurentius Lindoris* and *Richardus Corvellus*, Doctors of Law, and publick Professors of Philosophy

The College of St *Salvator*, commonly called the *Old College*, was founded by *James Kennedie*, Bishop of St *Andrews*, together with a Church beautified with a high tow'ring Steeple all of hewen Stone, in which his Monument of curious Workmanship is yet to be seen Mr *Skene*, Doctor of Divinity and Principal of the College, has of late repaired and augmented the Fabrick thereof, having made a Collection for that End He has also founded a *Library*, which by the Donations of Learned Men is now very well furnish'd with good Books

St *Leonard's* College was founded by *James Hepburn*, Prior of St. *Andrews*, in which are several Professors, as first the Principal, who is always Doctor of Divinity, and four Professors of Philosophy, to whom *John Scot* of *Scots Tarvett*, Kt added a Professor of Philology, with a liberal Salary, and augmented the Library with the Gift of several considerable Volumes.

It is likewise of late very much encreased by Sir *John Wedderburne*, Doctor of Physick, who dying, left his great Collection of Books to it Here also is the famous Manuscript of the *Scottish* Chronologer *John Fordon*

The *New College* was founded by *James Beaton*, Archbishop In it are two Professors, always Doctors in Divinity, the one stiled *Principal Professor of Theology*, the other only *Professor of Theology*, to which of late is added a Professor of Mathematicks, the first Professor whereof, Mr *James Gregory*, erected a commodious Observatory for Mathematical Observations in the College-Garden, having caus'd a Contribution to be made for that Purpose He also furnished it with many Mathematical Instruments much better than it had before his Time

Alexander the First, King of *Scotland*, founded a Priory here for the Monks of the Order of St. *Augustine*, the Government of the *Picts* being abolished in *Britain*, and *Kenneth* the Third transferred the Episcopal See from *Abernethie* to St. *Andrews*, about the Year 850.

De *ANDREAPOLI*, Carmen *JOANNIS JONSTONI*,

Quondam ibi Thologiæ Professoris.

IMminet Oceano paribus descripta viarum
Limitibus, pingui quam bene septa solo,
Magnificis opibus, staret dum gloria prisca
Pontificum, hic fulsit Pontificalis apex
Musarum ostentant surrecta palatia cœlo,
Delicias hominum, Deliciasq, Deum.
Hic nemus umbriferum Phœbi, Nymphæq, sorores,
Candida quas inter prœminet Urania,
Quæ me longinquis redeuntem Teutonis oris
Suscepit, excelso collocat inq, gradu
Urbs nimium fœlix, Musarum si bona nosset
Munera & ætherei regna beata Dei
Pelle malas pestes Urbe, & quæ noxia Musis,
Alme Deus coeant pax pietasq, simul

G L A S G O W.

GLASGOW is the most famous Empory of all the West of *Scotland* Notwithstanding that it is inferiour to many in Antiquity, yet if we respect the Largeness of the City, the Number and Stateliness of its publick and private Buildings, its Commerce with Foreign Nations, and the Opulency of its Inhabitants, it is the chief of all the Cities in the Kingdom next to *Edinburgh*

The City stands most pleasantly upon the East Bank of *Clyde*, which is navigable up to the very Town by Ships of small Burthen, but *New Glasgow*, which stands on the Mouth of *Clyde*, is a Haven for Vessels of the greatest Size The City it self is join'd to the Suburbs, which stand on the West Bank, with a beautiful Bridge of eight Arches, built of square hewen Stone

The most part of the City stands upon a Plain, and is in a manner four-square. In the very Middle of the City is the *Tolbooth*, magnificently built of hewen Stone, with a very high Tower, and Bells which sound melodiously at every Hour's End At the *Tolbooth* four principal Streets crossing each other do divide the City as it were into four equal Parts, every one of which is adorned with several publick Buildings

In the higher Part of the City the Cathedral Church stands, commonly called St *Mungo's*. It amazes the Eyes of the Beholders for its stupendious Bigness, and the Artifice of its Structure It consists of two Churches, of which the one is over the other The several Rows of Pillars, and exceeding high Towers, do show a wonderful Piece of Architecture

Near to the Church is the Archbishop's Castle, fenced with an exceeding high Wall of hewen Stone, and looks down to the City, but the chief Ornament of the City is the College, which was founded by King *James* the Second Pope *Nicholas* the Fifth granting an Indulgence, and confirming it by his Bull to have the Rights and Liberties of a College, where general Learning should be taught. It was erected by the great Labour and Expences of that Reverend Prelate *William Turnbull*, Bishop of *Glasgow*

The Words of the Bull for the Founding it are, That general Students should flourish in the same, as well in Theology, and the Canon and Civil Law, as in all other Arts and Faculties, and that the Masters and Teachers there should enjoy all and sundry the Privileges, Liberties, Honours, Immunities, and Exemptions which have been granted by the Apostolick See, or others, any other way, to the Masters, Teachers, or Students of our College at *Bonania* The Fabrick of the College is remarkable, consisting of divers Courts The Fore-part of it towards the City is of an excellent Structure, being of hewen Stone The Precincts of the College are enlarged by some Acres of Ground, Purchased by some Money granted to it of late by the King and Estates of the Kingdom It is separated from the rest of the Town by an exceeding high Wall

ROBERTI MAGNI, M. D Carmen in insignia Civitatis *GLASGUÆ*

Salmo, Quercus cui insidet Rubecula avis, & Campana, & Annulus aureus salmonis ore exertus.

SALMO maris, terræque arbor, avis aeris urbi
Promittunt quicquid trina elementa ferunt.
Et campana (frequens celebret quod numinis aras
Urbs) superesse polo non peritura docet
Neve quis indubitet sociari æterna caducis
Annulus id, pignus conjugiale, notat.

Old A B E R D E E N.

ABERDEEN the Old is situated a Mile to the North of the New Town, commonly called *Bon-accord* It has its Name from its Situation, being placed at the Mouth of the Water of *Don*. The Name of the River sufficiently shews that the *Picts* who inhabited this Part of the Country were of a *Scythian* Descent, for the River which by the *Latins* is called *Danubius*, by the *Germans* is called *Dunave*, by the *Polonians Dunaum*, by the *Turks Tuna*, being of the very same Name with our *Don*

The River is remarkable for the Multitude of Salmon and Perches which are taken in it About Half a Mile from *Old Aberdeen* it hath a Bridge of one single Arch, which is both large and stately: It is made up for the most part of square hewen Stone, both the Ends of it being fixed on Rocks By its crooked Winding it breaks the Force of the Stream, so that Nature it self seems to have made Way for its Situation A little below it *Don* enters into the Sea

Above the Bridge two Miles, is a Heap of Stone artificially cast in the Mouth of the Channel for the easier catching of the Salmon It was the Bishop's Seat, and hath a Cathedral Church, commonly called St *Machars*, of a large and stately Structure, being built of hewen Stone by the several Bishops of that See It anciently consisted of two Ranks of Stone Pillars, another cross Church, and three Turrets, the greatest of which was the Steeple, which was set upon four Pillars of vaulted Works In the Church likewise was a Library, but about the Year 1560 it was almost wholly destroyed, so that the Ruins do now only remain

But

But the chief Ornament of this Town is the King's College, placed on the South Side of the Town, conspicuous beyond the rest of the Houses for the Neatness and Stateliness of its Structure. 'Tis inferior to no College in *Scotland* One Side of it is covered with Slate, the rest with Lead, the Church and Turret or Steeple are of hewen Stone The Windows were of old remarkable for painted Glass, and some Reliques of their ancient Splendor do yet remain Here is a fine Monument of Bishop *Elphingston*. The Steeple, besides others, hath two Bells of an extraordinary Bigness The Top of it is vaulted with a double cross Arch, above which is a King's Crown, having eight Comets upheld by as many Pillars of Stone, a round Globe of Stone with two gilded Crosses closing the Crown In the Year 1631 it was overturned by a Storm, but shortly after was built in a more stately Form It was begun by Bishop *Forbes*, continued by *William Gordon*, Doctor of Physick and helped on by the Largesses of several Noblemen and Gentlemen of that Country Close to the Church there is a Library provided with many Books, much enriched by those which Dr *Henry Scougal*, Professor of Divinity there, and the Right Reverend Dr *Patr Scougal*, Bishop of *Aberdeen*, his Father, did lately bequeath to it

This College was founded by Bishop *Elphingston*, *Anno Dom.* 1500, and the greatest Part of the Work was likewise built by him, but King *James* the Fourth assumed the Patronage of it to himself, whence it is called the King's College In it there is a Primar or Principal, a Professor of Theology, a Professor of the Civil Law, a Professor of Physick, a Sub-Principal, who is also a Professor of Philosophy, three other Philosophy Professors, and a Professor of the Languages This College, and that in the New Town, make up one University, called the University of King *Charles*.

New ABERDEEN.

ABERDEEN, as I have said, is twofold, the New Town and the Old They are distant the one from the other about a Mile *Abredonia* seems to be the same which *Ptolomy* calls the City *Devana*, placed in the Province called *Texale*, upon the Mouth of the River *Dee*, for *Aber* in the old *British* Tongue signifies or denotes the Mouth of a River, and *Deva*, or *Dee*, is the Name of the River upon whose Mouth the City is situated But *New Aberdeen* is the Capital of the Sheriffdom of *Aberdeen*, and the Seat of the Sheriff for Tryal of Causes It is placed at the Eastern Corner of the Shire, where it is wash'd with the *German* Sea This City very much exceeds the rest of the Cities of the North of *Scotland* in Bigness, Greatness of Traffick, and Beauty It enjoys a wholesome Air, and abounds with well-bred Inhabitants, and hath a great Revenue from its Salmon-Fishing. The Old City seems to have been placed upon a Bank of the Sea, because it is the common Opinion, that the Monastery of the *Holy Trinity*, which is thought to have been formerly the Palace of King *William*, is situate in the very Creek of the Sea, and not far from it are the Ruins of an old *Pratorium* In Tract of Time the Inhabitants seem to have filled several neighbouring little Hills with Houses, and now the City is chiefly built upon Three of those Hills, and the greatest Part upon the highest. It hath an Access by an Ascent every way The exteriour Parts thereof are spread out upon the Plain, as Suburbs in many Places.

That there was a Mint heretofore in this City, appears by Silver Coins there stamp'd with this Inscription, *Urbs Aberdea*, which are yet preserved in the Closets of the Curious

The Streets are paved with Flint, or a very hard Stone resembling Flint the Houses beautiful both within and without, are four Stories high, or more, and have for the most part Gardens and Orchards belonging to them, so that the whole City, to those that approach it, gives the Resemblance to a Wood

At the West End of the City, a little round Hill adjoining offers it self to Sight, from the Foot of which Hill breaks forth a Fountain of clear Water, and in the Middle of the same another Spring, flowing down to the Foot of the Hill, bubbles out, and sends forth a Stream as rapid as a Torrent, but the Spring it self is easily distinguished both in Colour and Taste from the Torrent It is called the *Aberdonian Spaw*, because both in Taste and Quality it comes near to the *Spaw* Water in the Bishoprick of *Liege* This Water is cold to the Touch Doctor *William Barclay*, a Physician, has written a Treatise concerning it

In the High-Street there is a Church of the *Franciscans* worthy to be taken Notice of, built of Free-Stone, a Work begun by Dr *William Elphingston*, then Bishop, and finished at the Charge of *Gavinus Dumbar*, Bishop of *Aberdeen*, about the Year of Christ 1500

The said Bishop *Gavinus Dumbar* hath also got himself immortal Honour by a famous Bridge of seven Arches laid over the River *Dee*, about a Mile from the City, built very firm and durable of Free-Stone, which in more Places than one by Inscription testifies its Author or Builder

But the great Ornament of this City is its College, called the *Mareschallian Academy*, as founded by the Earl-Marshal, *George Keith*, in the Year 1593, which the City of *Aberdeen* hath very much adorned with several additional Buildings It has, besides a Primary Professor, who is called Principal, Four Professors of Philosophy, a Professor of Theology, and a Professor of the Mathematicks There is also a famous Library founded by the City of *Aberdeen*, supplied by the Gifts of learned Men, and furnished with divers Mathematical Instruments

Add to these the School-House founded by Dr *Dune*, which has one Head Master, and three Ushers under him There is also a School for Musick

The Cathedral Church nominated from St *Nicholas*, its Patron, is built of Free-Stone, and covered with Lead, has a Steeple resembling a Pyramid, and covered likewise with Sheets of Lead to a considerable Heighth It was divided formerly into three Churches, the biggest whereof was called the Old Church, the other the New Church, and the third the Arched, named the Arch of the Lady of Mercy. This Cathedral is propt with Pillars of Free-Stone, and has three Bells of a vast Weight, which by their quick and continual Sounds divide the half Hours The Body of this Church is adorned with a Tower and pinacled Steeple Here is kept the Court for the publick Tryals of the Townsmen, and the County Courts, where is also a Prison and a Work-House Besides these there is an Alms-House for the Maintenance of the old People of *Aberdeen* that are come to Decay, with three Hospitals founded by several Persons And adjoyning to the Custom-house lies the Port or Wharf.

De Abredonia Nova, Carmen D. J. JONSTONI.

AD boream porrecta jugis obsessa superbis
Inter Cognatas eminet una Deas
Mitior algentes Phœbus sic temperat auras,
Non æstum ut rapidum, frigora nec metuat
Fœcunda ditat Neptunus gurgite, & amnis
Piscosi gemmis alter adauget opes.
Candida mens, frons læta, hilaris, gratissima tellus
Hospitibus, Morum cultus ubique decens
Nobilitas antiqua, opibus submixa vetustis
Martiaque invicto pectore corda gerens
Justitiæ domus, & studiorum mater honoris
Ingenio ars, certant artibus ingenia
Omnia et cedunt meritos genetricis honores.
Pingere non ulla ars ingeniumve valet

HADDINGTON.

HADDINTON is situate on a pleasant Plain, on the Brink of the River *Tyne*, surrounded with several Noblemens Dwellings The most remarkable whereof is the House of *Yester*, the ordinary Mansion-House of the Marquis of *Tweddale* It is one of the pleasantest Seats, and hath the finest and greatest Planting about it in all *Scotland* Of old this Town was fortified by the *English*, several Vestigies whereof are yet to be seen

Here is a Church excellently built of hewen Stone, the Ruins whereof do testifie its former Splendour In a Chapel belonging to this Church there is an excellent Burial-place for the Chiefs of the Family of *Maitland*. Chancellor *Maitland* and his Lady, several others of the said Family, and the Duke of *Lawderdale*, are interred in this Place

It gives the Title of Earl of *Haddington* to a Branch of the House of *Hamilton*, who hath large Possessions and fine Seats hard by it

Henry Prince of *Scotland*, Son to St *David*, and *Ada* his Countess, founded a Nunnery in this Place

Within four Miles of *Edinburgh* the Earl of *Tweddale* hath another most pleasant House and Gardens, called *Pinkie* No Place in *Scotland* is surrounded with more little Towns and Houses of the Nobility and Gentry than this is, which appears chiefly from the House of *Stony-Hill*, where the Variety of so many Towns and Buildings, so great a Part of the Coast of *Lothian*, the River of *Forth*, and the Coast of *Fyfe*, give a most delightful Prospect

MONTROSS

A Town in the Shire of *Angus*, so called (as some think) from *Monrosi*, which in the ancient *British* Language signifies a Fennish Promontory, and was of old called *Celurca*

This Town is situated at the Mouth of the River of *Southesk*, on the North Side of it. It hath a Harbour for Ships of a considerable Burthen, and has frequent Correspondence with Foreigners, being adorned with fine Buildings of all sorts, and has an Hospital for the poorer Inhabitants

It gave the Title of Earl and Marquis to the Chief of the Family of the *Grahams*

De eadem Carmen *J. JONSTONI.*

AUreolis urbs picta rosis, Mons molliter urbi
Imminet Hunc urbi nomina facta canunt
At veteres perhibent quondam dixisse Cœlurcam
Nomine sic prisco & nobilitata novo est
Et prisca atque nova insignis virtute, Virûmque
Ingeniis, patriæ qui peperere decus

DUNKELL.

A Town in the Sheriffdom of *Perth*, on the North of *Tay*, at the Foot of the *Grampian* Hills, being surrounded with pleasant Woods It is the chief Market-Town of the *Highlands*, and was a Bishop's Seat The Ruins of the Cathedral Church are yet to be seen, but that which chiefly adorns it, are the stately Buildings lately erected by the Marquis of *Athol*, Father to the present Duke

DUMBLANE.

DUMBLANE is a pleasant litt'e Town, on the Bank of the River *Allan*, where the Ruins of the Bishops and Regular Canons Houses are to be seen Here the Lord *William Drummond*, Viscount of *Stathallan*, hath very fine Dwellings, and considerable Revenues in the circumjacent Country

Here also was a Church of excellent Workmanship, a part of which remains yet intire In the Ruins whereof is an ancient Picture representing the Countess of *Stratherne*, with her Children kneeling, asking a Blessing from St *Blanus* cloathed in his Pontifical Habit

Not long ago *Robert Lighton* was Bishop of this Place, a Man of an Exemplary Life and Conversation. He was afterwards translated to the See of *Glasgow*, which he willingly resigned, and gave himself wholly up to the Exercises of a pious and contemplative Life.

At his Death he left all his Books, both Manuscripts and others, to the Use of the Diocese of *Dumblane*, and mortified a Sum of Money for erecting a Library A Salary was also mortified to the *Bibliothecarius* by the same Bishop's Sister's Son. It gives the Title of Viscount of *Dumblane* to the Family of the Duke of *Leeds*, in *England*

HAMILTON.

HAMILTON is a Town of the Lower *Clidsdale*, situated in a most pleasant Plain upon the Western Bank of the *Clyde* Its chief Ornament is the Palace of the Duke of *Hamilton*, the Court whereof is on all Quarters adorned with most noble Buildings, especially the Frontispiece looking toward the East is of excellent Workmanship, and has a magnificent Avenue Upon the

the one Hand of this Avenue there is a Hedge, and on the other fair large Gardens, abundantly furnished with Fruit-Trees and pleasant Flowers of all sorts.

Upon the West Side of the Town there is a large Park, surrounded with a very high Stone Wall, which is about Seven Miles in Circuit, the Brook *Aven* running through it.

This Park is also famous for its Forest of tall Oaks, and for the great Number of Harts and Buffles it abounds with.

There is a Church adjacent to the Palace, in the Vaults whereof is the Burial place of the Dukes of *Hamilton*

This is the Place which gives both Name and Title of Duke to the Ancient, Great, and Illustrious Family of *Hamilton*, and the Town is well built

AIRE, or *AIRTH*

AIRE, an ancient Town, and the chief Market-place of the West of *Scotland*, excepting *Glasgow* In it the Sheriff Courts are kept, it being the head Town of that Sheriffdom, which bears the same Name It was of old called St *John's* Town, but now that Name is antiquated

This Town though it be situated in a sandy Plain, yet it hath pleasant and fruitful Fields, and Greens equally pleasant both Summer and Winter It hath a stately Church, and a Bridge with four Arches joins it to the *New Town*, which is situated on the North Side the Water, where is to be seen the Castle of the Laird of *Craigwallace*

A Mile North of the Town, not far from the Sea Shoar, there is a *Lazer-Hous*, commonly called the *King's Chapel*, which King *Robert de Bruce* set apart for maintaining *Lepers*

This Town, by the King's Patent, is the Sheriff's Seat, and hath Thirty two Miles to the South and North within its Jurisdiction

De *Aira*, Carmen *ARCTURI JONSTONI*

URBS cœli contenta bonis, vel ab aere puro
Vel quo forte cluis nomen ab ære trahis
Mole quidem parva es, sed molem dotibus auges,
Urbibus & magnis nobilitate pares,
Grandia saxa vides, exili corpore gemmas,
Plus tamen exilis gemma nitoris habet
Et Jovis exiguo surgit de semine Quercu,
Et septemgemini fluminis ora latent
Misse animis terras sibi quæ subjecit & undas
Tibridis urbs, olim nil nisi villa fuit

DUNOTTER

IT lyes in the Shire of the *Merns*, and is situated upon a high and inaccessible Rock stretch'd out into the Sea, and fortified with strong Walls It is one of the Dwellings of the *Earls Mareschal*, the Chief of the *Keiths*, who, for the Warlike Valour of their Predecessors in defending their Country from foreign Enemies, were made Hereditary Mareschals of *Scotland*

DRYBURGH

THE Abbey of *Dryburgh* is situate upon the Bank of the River *Tweede* in *Teviotdale* 'Twas founded by *Hugh de Morvill*, High Constable of the Kingdom of *Scotland*, for the Monks of the Order of *Premontre*

INVERNESSE.

THE head Town of the Sheriffdom of *Invernesse*, and the Sheriff's Seat, where he keeps his Court It is most commodiously situated on the South Side of the Water of *Nesse*, on the very Brink of the River, a fit Place for entertaining Commerce with the neighbouring Places

Of old it was the Seat of the Kings of *Scotland*, and has a Castle standing on a pleasant Hill, having a large Prospect into the circumjacent Fields and Town

Near the Castle there is lately a Bridge built over the Water of *Nesse*, consisting of Seven Arches all of hewen Work

It hath a Harbour fit for smaller Vessels, as also Two Churches, the one for the *English*, and the other for the *Irish*

De *Innernessa*, Carmen *ARCTURI JONSTONI*

URBS vicina freto, tu surgis in ubere campo,
Et prope Parrhasiæ Virginis ora vides
Atria te Regum decorant, & sanguine fuso
Pictorum, toties qui rubuere lacus
Vela ferens Nessus vitreis interluit undis
Et ratibus famulas applicat ille rates
Non coit unda gelu, medio sed tempore brumæ
Libera victrices in mare volvit aquas
Nec desunt gravidæ gelido sub sydere messes,
Nec minus est famuli fertilis unda freti
Proxima te Thule vicinaque ditat Ierne,
Omnis & arctoa insula septa vadis
Abstulit imperii dudum Bodotria fasces,
Et Dominæ titulo cœpit Edina frui
Tu tamen en patrium regni dicere, honorem,
Hunc natura tibi dat geniusque loci.

SCOON

SCOON is a Town in the Sheriffdom of *Perth*, famous in former Ages for the Abbey which was founded by King *David* the First for the Monks of the Order of St *Augustin* It is situated on the North Bank of the *Tay*, and is thought to be the Center of the Kingdom

Here is a Church, famous for the usual Coronation of the Kings of *Scotland*, in which is the Tomb of *David Murray*, who was the first of the Family of *Balvaird*, and was made Knight-Baronet by King *James* the Sixth, who also erected stately Buildings here, which are possess'd by his Heirs, under the Title of the Viscounts of *Stormont*

ELGIN

A Town in the Shire of *Murray*, or *Elgin*, situated on a pleasant Plain It was a Bishop's Seat, and the head Town of that Sheriffdom Upon a sandy Hill to the East of the Town are to be seen the Ruins of an old Castle It had a Cathedral Church of admirable Structure, as appears by the Walls and Ruins which are yet extant

It gives the Title of Earl of *Elgin* to the Family of *Ailsbury* in *England*, a Branch of the Family of *Bruce* in *Scotland*.

De *Elgina*, Carmen ARCTURI JONSTONI.

Laudibus Elgini cedunt Peneia Tempe
Et Bajæ veteres, Hesperidumque nemus
Hinc Martis, inde vides prædivitis æquora Campi
Frugibus hæc populum, piscibus illa beant
Huc sua Phæaces miserunt poma Damasci
Pruna nec hic desunt, vel Cerasuntis opes.
Attica mellificæ liquistis tecta volucres;
Et juvat hic pressis cogere mella favis
Æmulus argento fæcundos Loxa per agros
Errat & obliquis in mare serpit aquis
Arcibus Heroum nitidis urbs cingitur, intus
Plebei radiant nobiliumque lares
Omnia delectant, Veteris sed rudera Templi
Dum spectas, Lachrymis, Scotia, tinge genas

DUNDEE.

A Town in the Shire of *Angus*, so called from *Dun*, which in our old Language signifies a Hill, and *Tay*, the Name of a River, it being situated at the Foot of a Hill on the North Side of the River *Tay*, not far from its Entry into the Ocean

It stands on a most pleasant Plain, and is adorned with excellent Buildings of all Sorts, It hath two Churches, a high Steeple, a Harbour for Ships of Burthen, and a considerable Traffick with Strangers, whence the Inhabitants are generally rich, and those who fall into Decay have a large Hospital provided for them

Of old this Town gave the Title of Earl, and Dignity of Constable to the Chief of the *Scrimgers*, but of late it gave the Title of Viscount to the Lord *Dundee*, who was killed by their Majesties King *William* and Queen *Mary's* Forces at the Battle of *Gillicrankie*

De *Taoduno*, Carmen J JONSTONI

QUA Notus argutis adspirat molliter auris,
Hac placide coeunt Taus & Oceanus
Hic facile excipiens lenientes littore puppes
Inde genis vasti distrahit Orbis opes
Sæpe dolis tentata & belli exercita damnis,
Invictis animis integra præstat adhuc
Fama veteris crevit cum religione renata,
Locis & hinc fulsit pura nitela aliis.
Alectum dixere prius, si maxima spectes
Commoda, fors donum dixeris esse dei
Tu decus æternum gentisque urbisque Botti
Cætera dic patriæ dona beata tuæ

ABERBROTHOCK

ABERBROTHOCK, or *Arbroth*, is a Town of *Angus*, so called from *Aber*, which in our ancient Language signifies a Side or Bank and *Brotlock*, the Name of a Water which runs by it It lyes on the Sea side near the Promontory called *Red-Head*, and has a Harbour for Ships.

Here was one of the richest Monasteries of this Nation, founded by King *William* of *Scotland* about 1170, in Honour of *Thomas Becket*, Archbishop of *Canterbury*, with whom he was intimately acquainted It had several considerable Donations from *Gillcrist* Earl of *Angus*, and his Son *Gillbred* It was possess'd by the Monks of St *Bennet*, to the Inhabitants of which Town, for the Monastery's sake, at the Request of the said King *William*, King *John* of *England* granted the same Privileges and Liberties through all the Kingdom of *England* (except *London*) which the Natives did enjoy The Patent is yet to be seen among the Records of *Arbroth*

CORSREGAL, or *Reul's-Cross*.

THIS Monastery (an ancient but stately Edifice) lyes in the Shire of *Carrick*, and was founded by *Dunkan* Earl of *Carrick*, for the Use and Conveniency of the *Cistercian* Monks.

CHANNERIE.

A Town in the Shire of *Ross*, so called from the College of *Canons Regular* that flourished there, lyes on the Sea side, and is surrounded with pleasant Hills It had a large Cathedral Church, a Part of which doth yet remain, and was a Bishop's Seat

Here is to be seen a stately Dwelling of the Earl of *Seaforth*, who hath considerable Revenues in that Country

---

PERTH.

THE head Town of the Sheriffdom of *Perth*, and the Sheriff's Seat where he keeps his Courts. For Dignity it is the second Town in *Scotland*, and is commonly called St. *John's Town*, from a Church built there, and dedicated to St *John*

It is a pretty Town, placed between two Greens on the South Bank of *Tay* At a full Tide small Vessels may come up to the Town Of old it had a Bridge of Stone, which was carried away by an Inundation Here was also a famous Monastery founded by King *James* the First, *Anno Dom* 1430, for the *Carthusians*.

It gives the Title of *Earl* to the Family of *Perth*, Chief of the Name of *Drummond*

De

De *Pertho*, Carmen *J JONSTONI*

Propter aquas tui liquidas & amæna vireta
Obtinet in medio regna superba solo
Nobilium quondam Regum clarissima sedes;
Pulchra situ, & pingui germine dives agri
Finitimis dat jura locis, moremque modumque
Huic dare, laus illis hæc meruisse dari
Sola inter patrias incincta est mænibus urbes,
Hostibus assiduis ne vaga præda foret
Quanta Virum virtus, dextræ quæ præmia norunt
Cimber, Saxo ferox, & genus Hectoridum
Fælix laude nova, fælix quoque laude vetusta
Perge recens priscum perpetuare decus

DUMFERMELIN

A Town situated on the West End of the Sheriffdom of *Fife* It was of old the King's Seat For on a little Hill near the Bridge are to be seen the Ruins of an old Castle, which is supposed to have been the Palace of *Malcolm Canmoir* It hath a Royal Palace in it, near to which are the Ruins of a stately Monastery, which was founded *Anno* 1130 by *David* I. King of *Scotland*, for the *Benedictine* Monks, and finished by King *Malcolm* III. where also both he and St *Margaret* his Queen are buried It is famous for the Birth of King *Charles* I and gives Title of Earl to a Branch of the Family of the *Seatons*.

CULROSSE

HATH its Name from *Cul*, which signifies a Bank or Border, and *Rosse*, which was the ancient Name of *Fife*, because it lyes in the Western Corner of that Shire

It is situated on a Descent at the Side of the River of *Forth*, its chief Commodities being Salt and Coals That which chiefly adorns it, is the stately Buildings of the Earl of *Kincardin*, with the Gardens and Terrace-walks about it, having a pleasant Prospect from *Sterling* to the very Mouth of the River *Forth* Near unto these Buildings are to be seen the Ruins of an ancient Monastery

KELSO

A Town in *Teviotdale*, situated on the North Side of the River *Tweede* It was lately almost wholly destroy'd by Fire, but is now rebuilt and adorned with most stately Buildings It is surrounded with several Noblemens Manors, and most pleasant and fruitful Fields

Here are to be seen the Ruins of an ancient Monastery founded by King *David*, and possess'd by the *Cistercian*, an Order instituted about the Year 1000 under Pope *Urban* the Second, by *Robert*, Abbot of the famous Monastery of *Cisteaux* in *Burgundy*, whence the Observers of that Order were called *Cistercians*

The Castle of BOTHWELL

IN Lower *Clidsdale*, not far from the River *Clyde*, near to which is a Bridge of hewen Stone The Ruins of the Castle only are to be seen, which notwithstanding do testify its former Greatness

Here of old was a Prebendary enjoy'd by a Secular Priest, founded by *Archibald* Lord *Douglas*

MELROSSE

IT lyes in *Teviotdale*, on the Bank of the River *Tweed*, was founded by St *David* in the Year 1136, and possessed by the *Bernardine* Monks, so called from St *Bernard* a *Burgundian*, who entring the Monastery of *Cisteaux*, proved so strict an Observer of Monastick Discipline, that the Regulars of the foresaid Order took their Name from him, and are called at this Day promiscuously *Bernardines* or *Cistercians*

BRECHIN

BRECHIN is a Town situated upon the Banks of the Water of *Southesk* in the Shire of *Angus*, and was a Bishop's See Here is a stately Bridge over the River *Esk*, consisting of Two Arches It is a considerable Market-Town for Salmon, Horses, Oxen, and Sheep Here also are to be seen the Ruins of the Bishop's Paface, and of the Canons Houses. *Brechin* likewise is famous for a memorable Slaughter of the *Danes*, not far from it

De *Brechina*, Carmen *ARCTURI JONSTONI*

Fertile Brechinum geminos interjacet amnes
Hic Boream spectat, respicit ille Notum
Rupibus inclusæ sternuntur pontibus undæ
Sunt quoque securis flumina plena vadis.
Hanc simul Arctoi decorat victoria Regis
Perfida cum socii terga dedere Duces
Præsulis hic sancti domus est, & pyramis ædi
Proxima, Phydiacæ forsitan artis opus
Si molem spectes, nihil est exilius illa,
Ipsa tamen cæli culmina tangit apex
Est structura teres, nec raro lumina fallit,
Eminus hanc spectans esse putabis acum
Dædala compages est, & ventos videt & imbres,
Nec metuit magni tela trisulca Jovis
Si fabricam conferre lubet, Brechinia turris
Pyramidas superat, Nile superbe, tuas.

ROSLIN

ROSLIN-Chapel

THis Chapel lyes in *Mid-Lothian*, four Miles from *Edinburgh*, and is one of the most curious Pieces of Workmanship in *Europe* The Foundation of this rare Building was laid *Anno* 1440 by *William St Clair*, Prince of *Orkney*, Duke of *Holdenburgh*, &c a Man as considerable for the publick Works which he erected, as for the Lands which he possess'd, and the Honours which were confer'd upon him by several of the greatest Princes of *Europe* It is remarkable that in all this Work there are not two Cuts of one Sort. The most curious Part of the Building is the Vault of the Quire, and that which is called the *Prince's Pillar*, so much talk'd of This Chapel was possess'd by a Provost, and Seven Canons-Regular, who were endow'd with several considerable Revenues, thro' the Liberality of the Lairds of *Roslin*.

Here lyes buried *George* Earl of *Cathness*, who lived about the Beginning of the Reformation, *Alexander* Earl of *Sutherland*, Great Grand-Child to King *Robert de Bruce*, Three Earls of *Orkney*, and Nine Barons of *Roslin*

The last lay in a Vault so dry, that their Bodies have been found entire after Fourscore Years, and as fresh as when they were first buried There goes a Tradition, that before the Death of any of the Family of *Roslin* this Chapel appears to be all on Fire

PASLEY.

A Monastery in the Barony of *Renfrew*, founded by the Steward of *Scotland* in the Year 1160 The Monks of *Clugny* were the first Possessors thereof, then the *Cistercians*, and after that the Monks of *Clugny* a second time, who were religious Persons of the Order of St *Bennet*, but reformed by *Odo*, Abbot of *Clugny* in *Burgundy*, from whence they had their Name

The Monks of this Place wrote a History of this Nation, commonly called *The Black Book of* Pasley At the Reformation it was bestowed on the Duke of *Chattelherault* Sir *Robert Spotswood* had this Book in his Library, and after he was executed, General *Lambert* got it, and brought it to *England*.

The BASSE.

IS a little Island within the *Forth*, about a Mile distant from the South Shore The Prospects of it sufficiently testifie how difficult the Access to it is.

Upon the Top of this Island there is a Spring, which sufficiently furnishes the Garrison with Water, and there is Pasturage for Twenty or Thirty Sheep. 'Tis also famous for the great Flocks of Fowls, which resort thither in the Months of *May* and *June*, the Surface of it being almost covered with their Nests, Eggs, and young Birds The most delicious amongst these different Sorts of Wild-Fowl is the *Solan Goose* and the *Kittie-Waicke* There is only one Island more in the West of *Scotland*, called *Ailsey*, where these Geese do breed; and from these Two Places the Country is furnished with them during the Months of *July* and *August* This Island of the *Basse* was an old Possession of the Family of *Lauder*, and in King *Charles* the Second's Reign it was bought and annex'd to the Crown.

FINIS

Printed for *Andrew Johnstone* and Sold by him at the *Golden Eagle* in *Old Round Court*, *Strand*.

Prospect of Edinburgh from ye North

...is Plate is Most humbly Inscrib'd to the Most Hon[ble] the Marques of T...

nnandale Earl of Hartfield &c Lord Privy Seal for the Kingdom of Sc
Majesties Most Honourable Privy Council and K

land Ld Lieutenant of y^e Shires of Dumfries & Pebells & Steuartry of Kircudbr
ht of the Most Auncient & Noble Order of y^e Thistle

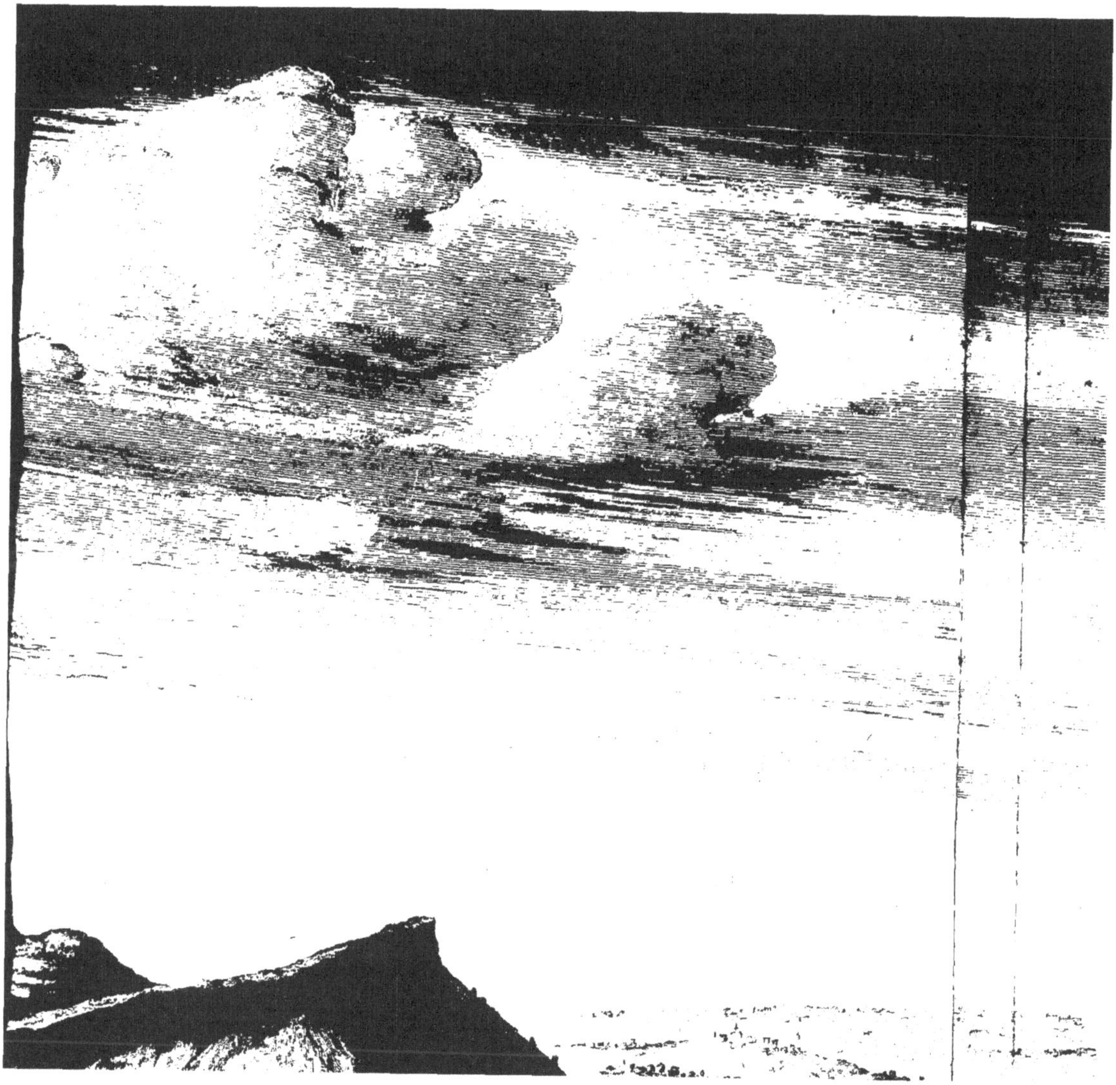

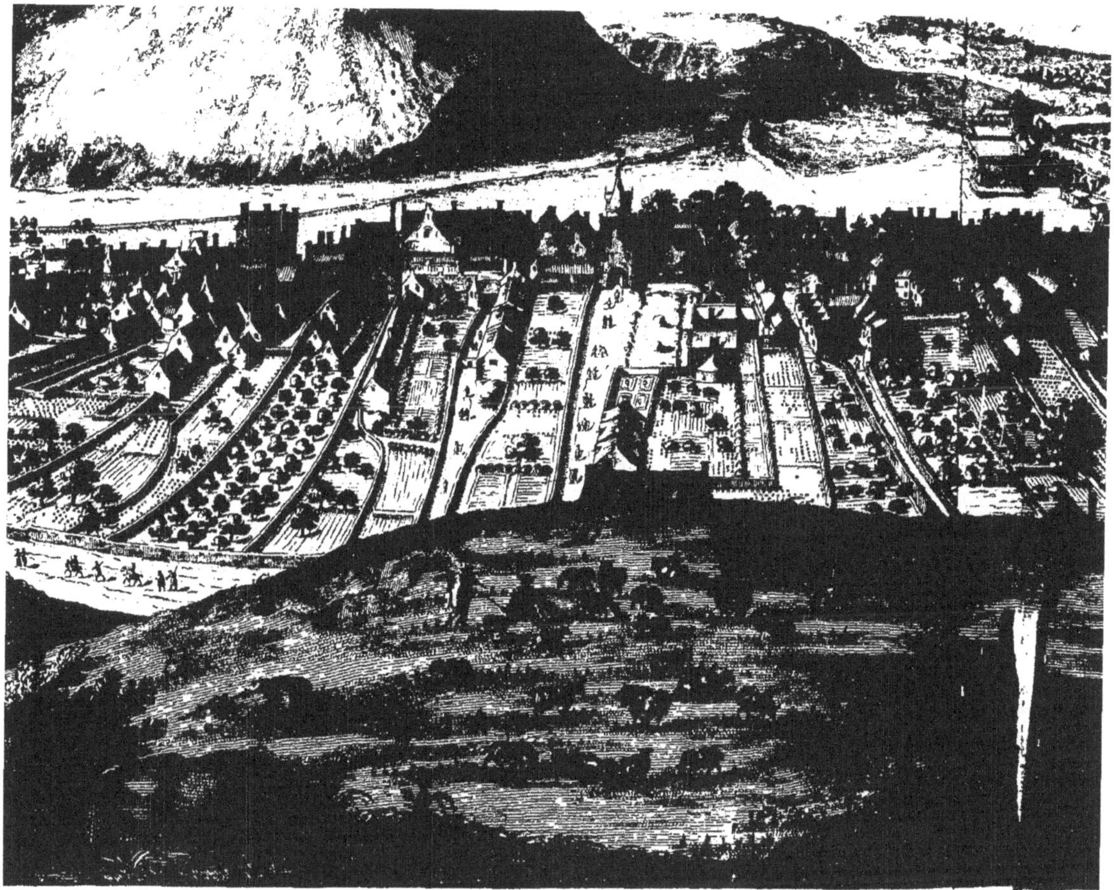

le Earl of Hartfield &c. Lord Privy Seal for the Kingdom of Scotland
Majesties Most Honourable Privy Council and Knight of

Ld Lieutenant of ye Shires of Dumfries & Pebells & Steuartry of Kircudbright:
the Most Auncient & Noble Order of ye Thistle

Steuart Principall of ye Stewartry of Annandale & Kircudbright One of His

The North-East View of

EDINBURGH CASTLE.

Facies Arcis EDENBURGEENÆ Th

This Plate is Most humbly Inscribd To ye Honble Sr George Warrender of Lochend Bart Who Sa
in Parliament for the said City

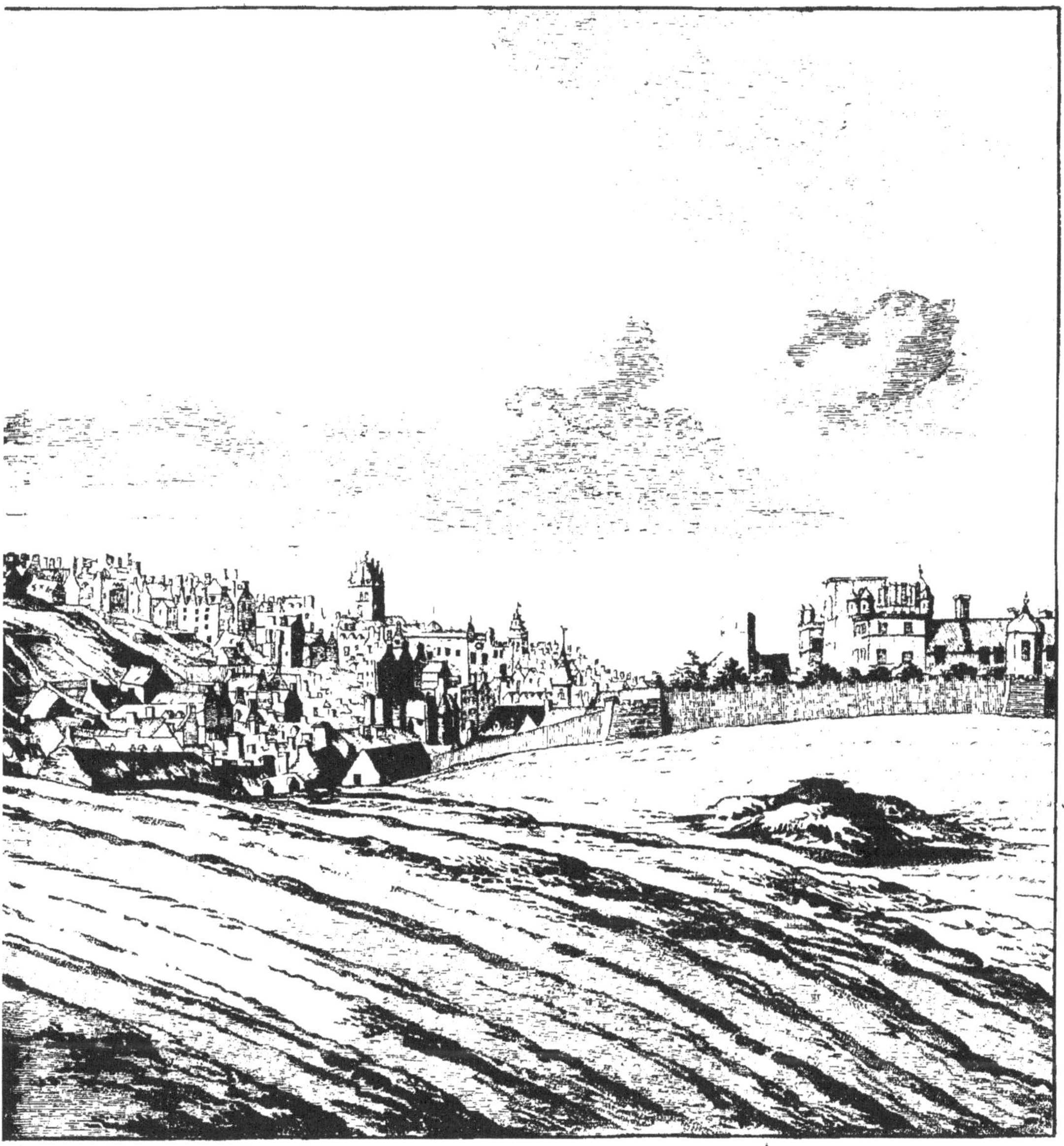

Southside of the Castle of EDINBURGH.

Ly Town of Edr in ye Station of Th. faus or Baillie Dean of Guild Provost and Present representative

Prospectus Civitatis EDINBURGENÆ a prædio DE
This plate is most humbly Inscrib'd to ye Honble Sr James Steuart of Goodtrees Bart His Maj

2

N dicto. The Prospect of EDINBRUGH from ye DEAN

res Solicitor Generall for Scotland & representative of ye said City in the last Parliament of Queen ANN

Arx BRITANNODUNENSIS ab Oppido Cella Patric

(This plate is most humbly Inscrib'd to the Honble Sr Robert Pollok Bar^t. Coll

dicto . The Castle of DUMBRITTON from Kilpatrick
l and Governour of Forth William

Prospectus Arcis Regiæ BRITANNODUNENSIS ab Occidente

This Plate is Most humbly Inscribed To John Haldane of Gleneagles One of th

Their Ma[ties] Castle of DUMBRITTON from the West

Honourable Comissioners of Police and Customs for North Britain 4

Facies Arcis BRITANNODUNENSIS *ab Oriente.* Th

(This plate is most humbly In[illegible] to the Right Ho

Prospect of y^e Castle of DUMBRITTON from y^e East
the Lord Forrester &c.

5

The Prospect of the Town of Sterling from the East.

URBIS *STERLINI*, PROSPECTUS AB ORIENTE.

The Prospect of their Maties Castle of Sterling.

ARCIS REGIÆ STERLINENSIS PROSPECTUS.

The Prospect of Sterling Castle

The Prospect of the House, & of the Town of Allou

The plate is most humbly inscribed to the Hon.ble James Arskine of Grange Esq.r One of

PROSPECTUS ARCIS, ET OPPIDI DE ALLOÂ.

rators of the colledge of Justice 8.

Prospectus Civitatis LIMNUCHI . Th
(This plate is most humbly Inscribed to The Right

Prospect of the Town of LINLITHGOW.
...on^ble the Earl of Hopton &c^a

Prospectus Regis Palatii LIMNUCHENSIS. Th

(*This plate is Most humbly Inscrib'd to the Ri*

e Profpect of Their Maj[ties] *Palace of* LINLITHGOW

Sr *James Cunynghame of Milncraig Bar*[tt]

10

Prospectus FALCOLANDIÆ ab Oriente

This plate is Most-humbly Inscrib'd to The Right Honble the

he Prospect of FALKLAND from the East .
iscount Falkland

Prospectus FALCOLANDIÆ ab Oriente Th
This plate is Most-humbly Inscrib'd to The Right Honble the

. Prospect of FALKLAND from the East

ount Falkland

Palace

FALKLAND

Ruderæ Ecclesiæ Cathedrælis Sancti ANDREÆ

(This plate wth the following Wiews of ye Cathedralls are most humbly Inscribd to The Right &c

The Ruins of the Cathedrall of St ANDREWS.
nd Father in God William Ld Bishop of Carlyle Lord Almoner to His Majestie 14

Rudera Arcis Sancti ANDREÆ

This plate wth ye following Prospect of the City of St Andrews is Most humbly Inscrib'd to the Rig...

e Ruins of the Castle of S^t. ANDREWS

John Earl of Rothess &c.^t Lord Vice Admirall of North Britain & Governour of Sterling Castle

Facies Civitatis Sancti ANDREÆ *Th*

Prospect of The Town of St ANDREWS.

Facies Civitatis GLASCOÆ ab Austro   The pro

spect of the Town of GLASGOW from yͤ South .

Facies Civitatis GLASGOW ab Oriente Estevo Th

Prospect of ye Town of GLASGOW from ye North East

The COLLED

f GLASGOW

Facies Civitatis Novæ ABREDONIÆ ut a propugnaculo Blockhousi

This plate is most humbly Inscrib'd to the Right Hon.ble

aspicitur *New ABERDENE from the Block houses*
Lord Hadd:

Facies Civitatis ABERDONIÆ Veteri

This Plate is Most humbly Inscribed to The Rt. Honble Sir ...

The Prspect of Old ABERDIEN.

Lord Lovat &c— Governour of Invernesse

20.

Prospectus Civitatis HADINÆ. The Prospect o

This Plate is Most Humbly Inscribed To the Right Hon.ble Thomas

the Town of HADDINGTOWN

Haddington &c. Knight of ye Most Ancient and Most Noble Order of the Thistle

Prospectus Oræ maritimæ LOTHIANÆ a Prædio d

This Plate is Most Humbly Inscribd to the Right Honble S^{r} Da

ny hill *The Coast of LOTHIAN from Stony hill.*

Dalrymple of Hailes Bar.t Lord Advocat for Scotland. 22

Prospectus Civitatis MONTIS-ROSARUM

The Prospect of the town of MONTROSE

Prospectus Civitatis CALIDONIÆ

This Plate is Most Humbly Inscribed to The Rt Honble Lord James Murray

e Prospect of the Town of DUNKELD

utenant Colonel in His Majestys First Regiment of foot Guards 24

Ecclesia Cathedralis CALIDONIÆ

The Cathedrall Church of DUNKELI. 25

Prospectus Oppidi DUMBLANI

This Plate is Most humbly Inscribed To His Grace John Duke of

Prospect of the Town of DUMBLANE.

le &c. Knight of the Most Noble Order of the Garter 26

Ecclesia Cathedralis DUMBLANI

he Cathedrall Church of DUMBLANE

Prospectus Oppidi HAMILTONIÆ Th

This plate is Most Humbly Inscrib'd to Her Grace y Dutchess of Hamilton & B. adon &c.

Prospect of the Town of HAMILTON 28

ghter & Heiress to Dig y Lord Gerard of Gerards Bromley in the County of Staffo d

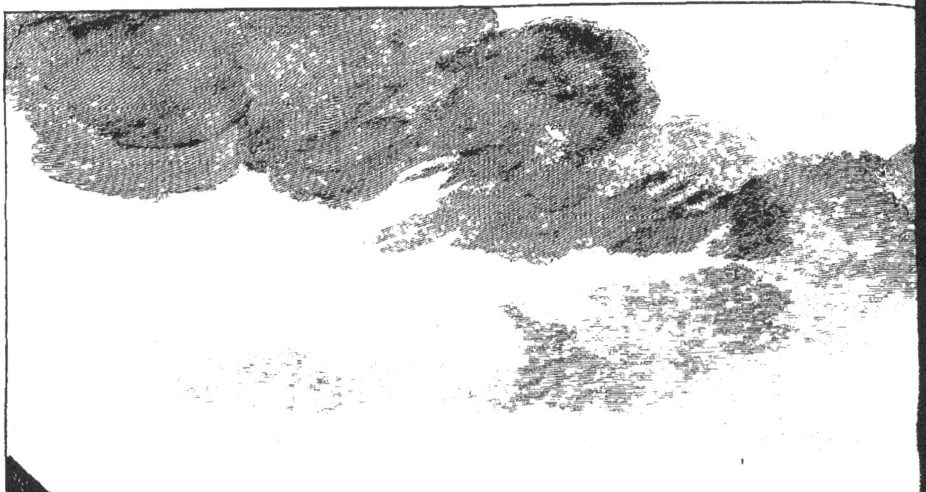

Prospectus Civitatis AERÆ ab Orientale . The
This Plate is Most Humbly Inscribed To the Rt Honble Alexander Lord Polwarth Envoy

Prospect of the Town of AIR from the East.

...rdinary & Plenepotentiary from ye King of Great Britain To ye King of Denmark & ye King of Prussia

Prospectus Civitatis AERÆ a Domo de Newtown

This plate is most humbly Inscribed to Sr Th

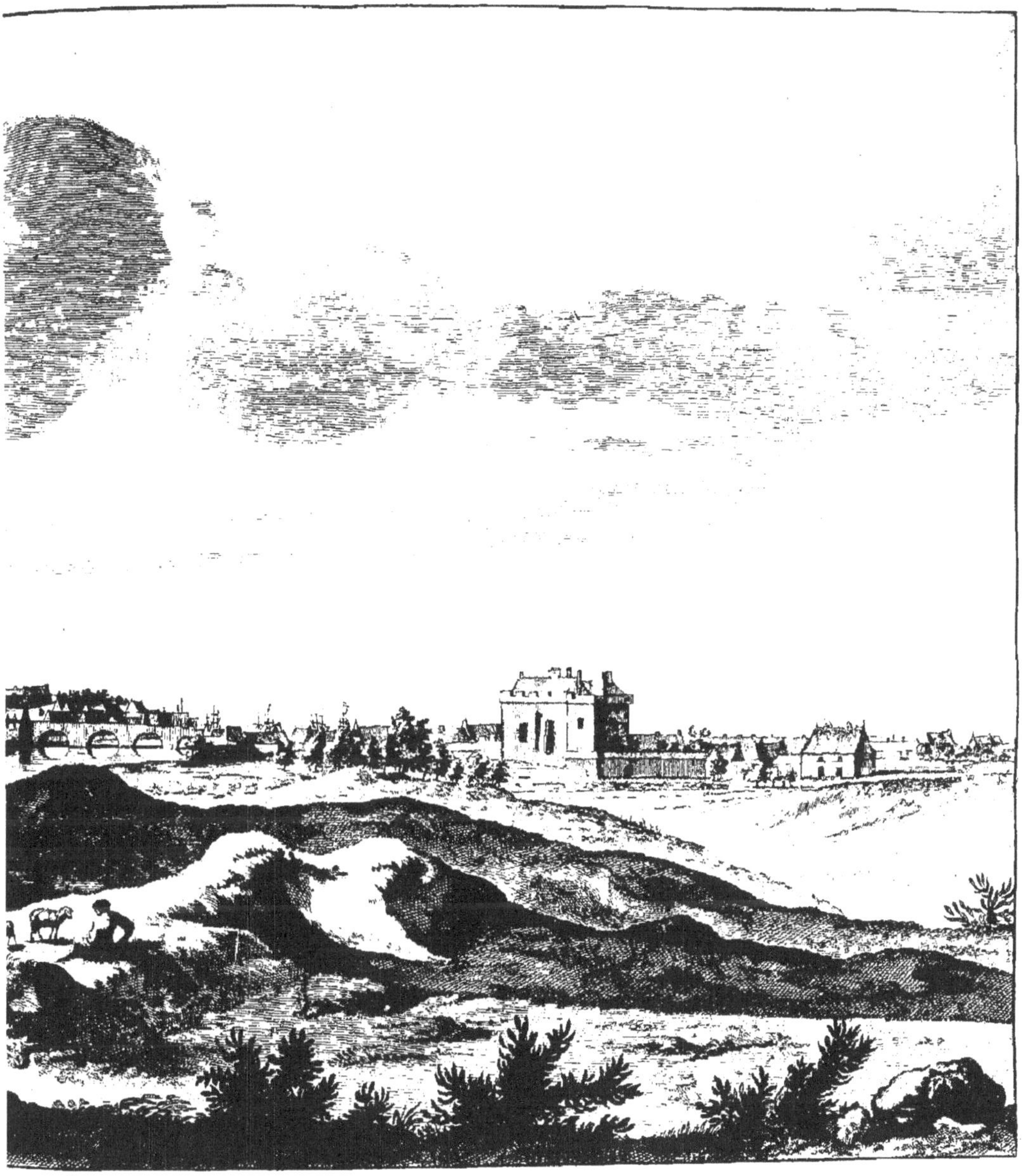

The Town of AIRE, from y^e House of Newtowne
Wallace of Craigy Bart

PROSPECTUS ARCIS DUNOTRIE

The Prospect of Dunotter Castle.

Prospectus Oppidi de DRYBURGH (

e Prospect of the Town of DRYBURGH.

Rudera Cœnoby de DRYBRUGH.

This Plate is most humbly Inscrib'd to ye Honble John

e. Ruines of the Abbey of DRYBRUGH
gle of Haining Esqr

Prospectus Civitatis INNERNESS.

This Plate is Most Humbly Inscribed To the Right Hon.ble John

Earl of Sutherland Heritable Admiral of ye Counties of Sutherland and Caithness Vice Admiral of the Stewartry of Orkney & Zetland Lord Lieutenant of ...

e prospect of ye Town of INNERNESS, 34

arl of Sutherland Ld. Strathnaver &c Heretable Sheriff Heretable Lord of Regality Heretable Crowner of y

s Elgine Nairne Cromertie Ross Sutherland and Caithness Stewartry of Orkney & Zetland President of y Court of Police in Scotland Lieutenal General of his Majesties Forces

Prospectus Palaty et Oppidi de SKUYN. Th
This plate is Most humbly Inscribed to The Honble James Murray Se

Prospect of the House and Town of SKUYN.

to the Right-Honble the Viscount of Storment

35

Prospectus Oppidi ELGINÆ

The Prospect of the Town of ELGINE

Rudera Templi Cathedralis ELGINI.

The

Ruins of the Cathedrall Church of ELGIN

Prospectus Civitatis TAODUNI

This Plate is most humbly Inscrib'd to Thom

e Prospect of y^e Town of DUNDEE
Paterson Esqr

38

Prospectus Civitatis TAODUNI ab Oriente

This plate is most humbly Inscrib'd to y^e Honble Coll William Ker Collonel of Her Royal Highness the D

The Prospect of ye Town of DUNDEE from ye East

…s of Waless Regiment of Dragoons & one of ye Grooms of the Bed Chamber to His Majestie 39

Prospectus Oppidi ABERBROTHIÆ. (Th

This plate is most humbly Inscrib'd to the Right Hon.ble the Ea

Prospect of y^e Town of ABERBROTHICK

f Northes k &c.

Prospectus Cœnoby ABERBROTHIÆ Th
(This plate is Most humbly Inscrib'd to The Hon

Prospect of ye Abby of ABERBROTHICK
[...]llonell Robert Murray

Rudera Cænoby de CORSREGAL seu crucis Sti Re
This plate is Most humbly Inscribd to William

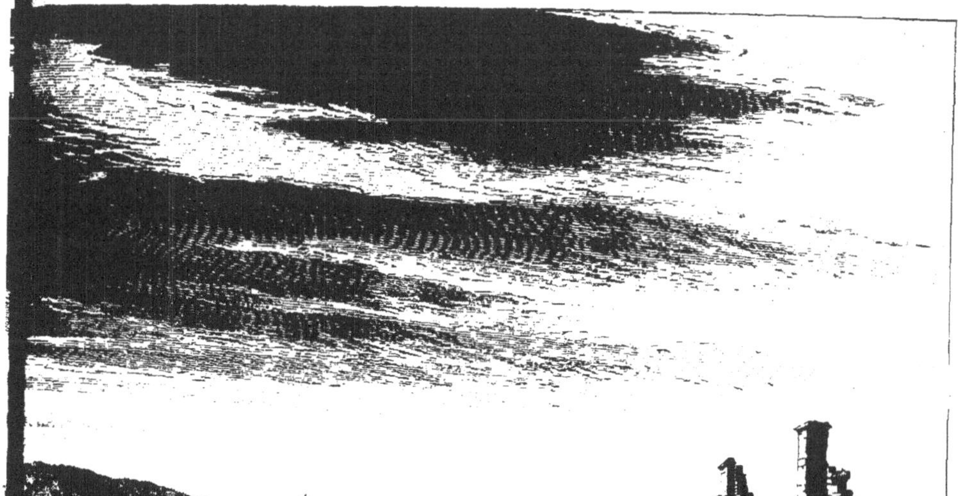

The Ruines of y^e Abby of CORSREGAL.

of Laureston Esqr

42

Chanonria Civitatis Rossiæ.

The CHANNERY Town of Ross.

Prospectus Civitatis PERTHI. T
This Plate is Most Humbly Inscribed To His Grace To

Prospect of ye Town of BERTH .
Duke of Argyle &c

Prospectus Oppidi et Cœnoby FERMELODUNENSIS

This Plate is Most Humbly Inscribed To the Hon[ble] Charles Cathcart Lieutenant Colonel of y Royal Re

The Prospect of y^e Town & Abby of DUMFERMLING.

of Grays Dragoons & One of The Grooms of y^e Bed Chamber to His Royal Highness y^e Prince of Wales 45

Prospectus Cenoby FERMELODUNENSI
This Plate is Most Humbly In...

The Prospect of the Abby of DUMFERMLING.

...d to The Right Hon.ble John Lord Lesley &c.

Prospectus Palatij & Oppidi CULROSSIÆ.

This Plate is Most— Humbly Inscrib'd to the Honble

e Prospect of yᵉ House & Town of COLROSS
lonel John Hope

Prospectus Cœnoby de CULROSS.

This plate is Most Humbly Inscrib'd To Alexan

e Prospect of the Abby of Culross
r Stuart. D.M. F.R.S.

48

Prospectus Oppidi CALSONIS

This Plate is Most Humbly Inscrib'd To His Grace John Duke of Roxburgh Marques of Bo…
of the Counties of Roxburgh & Selkirk, Lord Keeper of the Great Seal of Scotland and One of His Maj…

he Prospect of the Town of KELSO
umont & Cessfoord Earl of Kelso Viscount of Broxmouth Lord Ker Cessford & Caver to ... Ld Lieutenant
ester Most Honorable Privy Council

Monasterium Calsonens

This Plate is Most humbly Inscrib'd to John Inglis Esqr. N

E The Abby of KELSO
sistant Master of The Ceremonies

Prospectus Arcis BOTHWELIÆ

This plate is Most humbly Inscribed To the Honble Brigadi

The prospect of BOTHWELL Castle

Dalzel

Rudera Cœnoby de MELROSS,

The Ruines of the Abbie of MELROSS

Prospectus Oppidi BRECHINÆ (The
(This plate is Most-humbly Inscribd to the Honble Collonll

Prospect of ye Towne of BRECHIN.
n. Campbel

Capella de ROSSLIN

The Chappell of ROSSLIN.

54.

Prospectus Cœnoby et Civitatis PASLETI. (Pl...

This plate is most humbly Inscrib'd to The Right Honble the...

he Prospect of the Abbey & town of PAISLAY
Earl of Dundonald &c —

57.

Facies Insulæ BASSÆ ab ora Maris Australi

The Prospect of ye BASS from ye South shore

Latus Insulæ BASSÆ Orientale. Th

he East syde of the BASS

Lauder
This Plate Is Most humbly
Rt Honble Charles

Castle
Inscribed to the
Earl of Lauderdale &c.